INTRODUCTION

Friendly Street's 'New Poets' series began in 1995 to promote and encourage emerging South Australian poets.

This book brings to 27 the number of South Australian poets whose first collections have been published in the series. Many of the poets previously published have since published full-length collections, or become editors of literary magazines or poetry educators. And the number of submissions received for this book suggests that there are many more poets embarking on similar journeys.

This year's compilation is a wonderful surprise to me. I had not previously heard the voices of these three poets. None of them were regular or even occasional readers at Friendly Street. I was excited and delighted upon reading their poems for the first time. Here are three quite distinct perspectives, in which you will find delicacy, freshness, wit, playfulness, observation and, quite often, the unexpected. Many of the poems are open doors or windows. I invite you to step or look through them . . .

David Adès,
Convenor,
Friendly Street Poets

FRIENDLY STREET

new poets nine

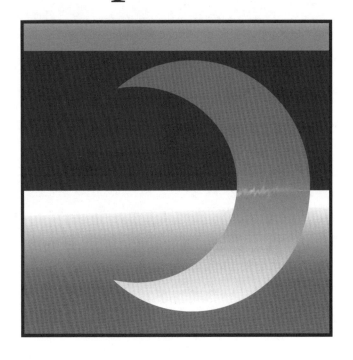

Peeling Onions Jill Gloyne

Crescent Moon Caught Me Judith Ahmed

Scoffing Gnocchi Linda Uphill

Friendly Street Poets

Wakefield
Press

Friendly Street Poets Incorporated
in association with
Wakefield Press
1 The Parade West
Kent Town
South Australia 5067

www.friendlystreetpoets.org.au
www.wakefieldpress.com.au

First published 2004

Cover illustration by Jonathon Inverarity
Designed by Gina Inverarity
Typeset by Clinton Ellicott
Printed and bound by Hyde Park Press, Adelaide

ISBN 1 86254 638 X

Wakefield Press thanks Fox Creek Wines
and Arts South Australia for their support.

CONTENTS

PEELING ONIONS

by Jill Gloyne

Jill Gloyne was born at Port Augusta and now
lives on Kangaroo Island. Her careers include:
nursing, bringing up five children, studying
French to the level of MA as a mature-age
student at Adelaide University, helping run a
farm on Kangaroo Island and now, in
'retirement', writing. In 1997 she published
"You just had to deal with it", a history of
women and health care on Kangaroo Island
and in 1999 she published a book of short
stories, *The Nautilus Shell ... and other tales*.
She has won numerous awards for short
stories and poems and been published in
various anthologies.

ACKNOWLEDGEMENTS

'Fishing at Chapman River' was published in
Five Bells Volume 9 no 1 Summer 2002.
'Song Without Words' was published in the
Kingfisher Collection, Karrinyup Writers' Club
Inc. 2003
'Making Bread' won the Ballaarat Writing
Council's inaugural Martha Richardson Medal
and Award 2003.

I would like to thank members of the
Dudley Writers' Group for their fellowship
over the past sixteen years, the staff of
the SA Writers' Centre for their
support and advice, and the tutors of the
Professional Writing AIT Arts Course at
the SA Institute of TAFE for their enthusiasm
and encouragement.

For Bill

CONTENTS

Fishing at Chapman River

Your cast
snaps at a patch of air
wrapping it around the line
in a sibilant sigh
that ends with a soothing plop
releasing thoughts
from below the surface

dappled sunlight
dances on the water
silver shards of fish
that are not there

all we catch
are half-remembered tales
hanging in the branches
of the ancient paper-barks
that trail like leaves
at the water's edge

it's not a day
for catching fish
but then we knew
it wasn't meant to be
the pleasure's in the chase
and not the capture

words we never speak
hang between our laughter
and the lip that sips the wine
a net for catching dreams

I know you will be back
you've left cockles in my freezer.

Orpheus and Eurydice

He
could not feel her eyes
upon his back,
so he turned.

She,
with wings of grace
brushing against desire,
reached towards
his backward glance
but slipped and fell
into a bowl of stars
where words did not exist.

Curve of her cheek
still lies between
the sickle moon
and a young man's dream.

Gift

You gave me
part of yourself,
held out,
like a child's treasure,
on a grubby palm.
I blinked
to see more clearly,
but as I did
you blew it away.

By the time
I found it again
you had tied it
so tightly
I could feel it
broken
inside.

Good Friday

I thought it was a game,
this slow progression
round the table
from chair to chair,
an endless chain of point
and counterpoint:
'I will, I won't,
I do, I don't,
never, ever, always.'

And then, one morning,
before the sun had laddered
the world with broken shafts,
that biblical cock,
the one that crows,
guided me
to the thirteenth seat.

On Visiting Dunblane Cathedral, 1996

A year after mind's madness
blew apart those sweet young years
in five unbelievable minutes,
these children are remembered
by flowers which should not
have been plucked from their roots,
which should have been gathered
by those they mourn, or left
to blossom in fields nearby.
In jars of plasma-coloured water,
they hold their heads erect, rigid
with the memory of lives
snapped and sapped away.
Letters from living children
talk candidly of heartache only
the very young can accept.
Carved into a heart of stone,
Massacre of the innocents
will not wear away.

Storm over Pink Bay

Anchored to
its moorings,
the building shudders
throughout its body
as if stuck on the reef
I can see off-shore.

On a nearby ridge
an army of trees
fights for survival
marching into battle
with trench-coats flapping
wetly at their feet.

Thermals, out of kilter,
abandon birds
to bare branches
stripped of shadow.
Lightning shatters the world
into colourless glass.

Next day,
the storm has collapsed,
its memory a grief
of thin wet skin
with nowhere
to wring itself out.

Sea Song

Take me down to the sea with you
and I will be your lover true.

So sang the whispering wind of dawn
so sang the moon to the dying morn
wake me,

take me down to the sea with you
and I will be your lover true.

Two kestrels rode on the ocean's breast
one kestrel wept when the other left
take me,

take me down to the sea with you
and I will be your lover true.

To the silver bells of the sea that rang
six dolphins danced, six dolphins sang
wake me,

take me down to the sea with you
and I will be your lover true.

The tide burst open along the shore
and love cried out do not for-
sake me,

take me down to the sea with you
and I will be your lover true.

Head over Heels

She wanted to write a poem so she went for a
walk in the woods to pick a bunch of flowers
which she placed end to end in a long sentence
that wandered on and on for ever and ever
Amen.

When she cut it out and held it up to the light
it fluttered in the breeze like a silk ribbon.
That is a beautiful thought, she said,
and cut it into short lengths,
placing them on the page
one after the other
in the right order
very neatly.
Then she signed it.

When he walked past
he stopped and read her poem.
Without a word
he picked up the scissors,
cut out the lines
and turned them upside down.

Before she could turn away
he gave her his eyes
so she could read it.
Ah! she smiled,
handing them back.
I see.

Let's not Compare

If you expect to read an English sonnet,
think again. Who wants to read iambic
pentameter today? Who gets their kicks
from fourteen lines, three stanzas and a couplet,
or has the time for regimented verse
demanding as it does so strict a rhyme,
a b a b and so on down the line
or *abba* which I know is even worse?
Poor Shakespeare wrote one hundred fifty four,
the lovesick coot. Was that the only way
that he could get a satisfactory lay,
to write all day and then re-write some more?
Today, amongst his fans, he'd have a ball;
with verse as free as love, he'd fuck them all.

Poetry Editor
Or: On the demise of the definite article

Like a man with a fetish,
through poem after poem
he ferrets them out,
ubiquitous culprits
that hide behind nouns
like recalcitrant adjectives
on every line.

'Out, out!' he screams
fanatically,
wielding his red biro whip
with cutting precision.

Like soldiers,
battle-scarred and weary,
they stagger, shame-faced,
to their Waterloo
and disappear,
to be eclipsed by syntax
or poetic licence,
while planning
their escape
to France.

Creamed Cheese

The moon is made of mozzarella.
Each month its brassy ring
like some celestial dinner gong
summons lovers to a feast
along the milky way.

Night by night
the heat of passion
melts its edges,
strand by sticky strand
it disappears
into the single string
of a hammock.

Time to milk the cow
again.

Just a Piece of Furniture

i

That's right. Sit on me,
like you always do. Just think
of your comfort, not of mine.
I do have feelings you know.
Jealousy tears me apart
each time you take cushions
from that smart settee to hide
my worn out contours.
Besides, their brilliance
overpowers my shabbiness.
It's cruel to criticise
what you neglect;
a bright new outfit
could so easily uplift me.

Just wait. I'm working
on a broken spring.
That should fix you.

ii

At last. I thought
you'd never come to bed.
Yes, I know I'm comfortable,
orthopaedically designed,
a spring in every step.
Two hundred and six
individual pieces
exquisitely articulated
take your weight upon me
night after horizontal night.

Ever thought of sleeping upright?

iii

You think
you've got me framed
but you're framed too.
I've got you covered
every time you pass me by.
Admit it. You need me
to see yourself
as others do.
Without me
you would not exist.

iv

I'm not, by nature, frigid,
just rigidly controlled.
Even though I lose my cool
each time you reach inside,
that, too, is control of a kind.

Were I to melt into your warmth
I'd start to propagate the rot
that I'm supposed to stop.
That cannot be. Our fate's decreed.
Each time you thaw my frozen tears
the freeze returns between us.

v

So, you can read me like a book.
Not surprising, considering
you've got me up against the wall.

Tell me, am I fact or fiction?
I need your help.
I do not know myself.

vi

Whatever you do
don't open me.
Darkness hides the
distance between us,
keeping your face
as it used to be.
I could paint it
from memory,
blindfolded.
Yes, I know
the drawstring works
but please, don't touch,
leave it as it is.
The blinding light
might change
our world forever.

vii

Last night
I didn't hear you pack your things
I didn't hear you tell me why
I didn't hear you.

This morning
I'm stripped bare of all
but hollow echoes,
empty hangers tremble
in their vacancy.

I cannot find my clothes.

Shadow Play

The day you lost your shadow
gathering clouds blocked out the sun.

Did you lose it accidentally
or was it by design?

When I found it hanging like a halo
you struck me to the ground with angry blows

and would not take it back.
Yet still it came, unbidden.

Now you pass with leaden steps
preceded by that elongated shape,

a weight so burdensome it seems
there is no lighter life for dreams.

Peeling Onions

I need to hone my sharpest blade
to peel away the outer skin
and feel its pure white heart,
but that is just the beginning;
with head averted
to avoid the fumes,
I slice and chop relentlessly
with the cutting edge of my pen,
weeping as I tear apart
the heart of the matter.

Coup de Téléphone

The telephone is not the place, the space, for this.
I need to see your eye, the why the lie. I miss
your smiling face, our laughing games.
If you had kept our rendez-vous, you
might have felt me soothe your pain, again,
with touch, such as we used to do,
but now we talk through air where there
are no familiar words to share,
just those that tear, ensnare.
I'm lost. The cost of love without the trust
is much too high, so try,
when I hang up as hang I must,
to understand it's more than just
a see-you-soon good-bye.

Strings

When you hooked up my skirt
to manipulate my movements,
did you think you could control me,
just like that, parting my legs
with your silken threads?

You made me sing and dance,
your fingers a question mark
under my skin, but did you think
my steps would follow yours
voluntarily?

I am no puppet mouthing
someone else's thoughts.
I sing my own song,
dance to my own tune,
no strings attached.

From a to u

The problem with our friendship,
she said, is the middle vowel.
You did not treat it with due care.
And when you lost a part of it,
Plato's pleasant harmony
turned into Pluto's deep despair.

Accents

When I read Ioana's poems
her accent shimmers
above her words
like the heady bouquet
of rich, red wine
matured for years
in old Romanian oak.
I sense the character
of struggling vines
fighting against all odds
to bring me this sweet offering
whose lingering aftertaste
entices me to reach for more.

When I fill Antien's mug
with sweet black coffee
her quaint pronunciation
skitters around the rim
waiting to laugh with me
at every sip.
I see her at her wheel
throwing lumps of clay
with Dutch precision,
my smile an echo of hers.
Deep down, I drink her mirth,
pour out a second cup.

When I relax at Yvonne's
scrubbed pine table,
her accent seasons
the food she serves
with the subtle essence
of secret recipes,
her laughter, flavoured
with hints of hard-won
smiles, wrinkles into
the walnut trees that
pepper her native Savoy.

The accents of my friends
pattern my day with song.

Song without Words

He was a simple man. Unversed. Or worse.
Illiterate. Barely articulate. Tripped over words
like stumbling blocks. Misread their meaning,
leaning as they did at awkward angles
in their sentences. Preferred to disentangle
fencing wire and fishing line,
not convoluted letters of the mind.

And yet, between his workman's hands there grew
a wordless song that flew each time he looked upon
 his life,
his wife. His eyes to hers wrote poetry he knew
she understood. No need for metre, assonance
 or rhyme.
No cause to write, recite, communicate by mail.
At night his fingers traced unwritten lines,
translating, as he went, his text to braille.

Treading Grapes

When your fingertips brush
the nape of my neck,
the liquid desire
of our first pressing
envelops me.

I savour this moment
like mellow wine
tended with care
by the warmth of your sun
and brought to me
from the cellar of your heart.

Delicious.

Golden Wedding

Throughout his life
the strains of Woody Herman
dogged his footsteps
like a tenacious shadow
dancing in and out
along the path
he trod with her
an echo to his heart.

As records go
he kept the beat
full well.

His quickstep,
after fifty years,
still leads her
to a lover's
rumpled sheet.

Pruning the Vine

His days are growing shorter. Every winter,
prunes his daughter's vine. Speaks not of love
but demonstrates in silence how to curve
with care the plant that once he grafted into

ancient stock; trellis-trains the frame
of younger years, nips in the bud all wayward
shoots, removes dead wood, supplies the food
for thoughts to blossom, for fire to flame.

His summer fruit drips honey on the vine,
sweetens hours spent in dappled shade,
sings the vintage in the vat and adds
youthful effervescence to his wine.

Love, rusted onto well-worn pruning shears
grows deeper with the weathering of years.

Sunday Lunch

Carved by a generation of homework,
like a re-surfaced Pompeii, the table
on the verandah is our meeting place.
As we gather for our meal, sunlight drips
through vines upon a nearby trellis,
glazing us with amber oil, its golden glow
distilled from leaves of our family tree.
Unspoken rituals simmer down the centuries:
mannerisms, recipes, the way we garden,
clean the house – because we've always done it so.
We pick the bones of history, sweet and succulent,
secure in the knowledge of who we are.
Year after year our children harvest seeds
we've sown, adding their own spice to flavour
future gatherings under the vines, different,
yet surprisingly like those which went before.

Churinga

I am sitting in the kitchen at the table
cutting up vegetables for soup,
but I am not cutting up vegetables
at the table where I am not sitting.
Someone else now owns this house.
They have modernised it:
brought the toilet inside
with their hygienic hands,
discarded friendly fireplaces
and the stove now uses
heat that can't be seen.
In fact they've dragged it,
struggling to remain itself,
into the twentieth century,
mod cons being such an asset.
In spite of them, I still empty
the wash up bowl on the garden
(they call it grey water now)
and two newspapers still heat
the water for my shower
with a roar that takes me back
to wooden bath mats, ice chests
and canvas water bags. My spirit
inhabits the soul of their house
but I do not disturb them.
They cannot see me. I belong
to a day when dawn walked down
the street with pint-sized steps,
leaving creamy milk in its wake
and yeast swelled with pride overnight,
and my heart still beats in time
to the chime of the hour on a wall
that held me in and let me out.

Mr Thursday

Standing in the tunnel
of yesterday's century,
outlined by light
that splits the house in two
from door to door,

an old man hitches to his armpits
trousers from a taller son,
khaki remnant of Tobruk,
reflected glory,
worn each day with pride.

After school he welcomes us
with eyes that listen,
ears that see the need
to show us how to earn
what can't be bought.

In scorching heat his water bag
gives cool and sweet a crystal
purified by wrigglers in the tank,
their ballet dance a question mark
of undecided commas.

His voice enfolds us
like the smell of home-made bread,
leaven rising imperceptibly
in the childhood tales he tells.
In later years,

through the lens of memory,
we focus on this wisdom
found amongst the mortar
crumbling from the cracks
between his words.

Shopkeepers in O'Connell Street
call him Mr Thursday;
like a well-oiled clock,
treasured for dependability,
his routine never varies.

The girl with peaches in her cheeks,
weighs out his fruit and veg
from a shopping list as neat
as invisible stitches
on worn elbows.

With string bags balancing his stride
he walks the scales of friendship
along the smile of the hour it takes
to pass one block of shops
and then another.

The spring in his step has sung
the song of the miles he's walked,
like a spontaneous chorus
reaching out to touch
more people than he knows

and like a well-pitched note,
echoing down the valley
of sharp recall,
his whistle summons
the ghosts of Thursday.

Making Bread

Sunlight, on its winter bias, scarves
her hair with bands of silver. Floured hands,
in ritual creation, sculpt the heart
of the world from a grain of wheat. Sand

metes out the time she needs to work her dough,
knuckling invisible points of air, again
and again, with expertise, to and fro,
back and forth, until it's ready. Then,

dividing it, she rolls out strips, plaits
them like her daughter's hair; the final glaze,
a smile from the yolk of the sun, a song that's
set to sing with the voice of warming rays.

She does not set the world on fire to prove
her worth. Proves it daily beside her stove.

CRESCENT MOON CAUGHT ME

by Judith Ahmed

Judith was born in Southampton, England, and immigrated to Australia in 1966. She has worked as a teacher in South Australia and Nigeria, where she lived for twenty years. Judith was a member of the writing circle of FOMWAN, (Federation of Muslim Women's Associations in Nigeria). She wrote articles, poems and short stories for FOMWAN's magazine, *The Muslim Woman*, which she also helped to edit. On a trip back to South Australia, from November 1993 to February 1997, Judith attended the Applied Writing program at Hamilton Senior Campus, and taught in government high schools in the northern suburbs. Her poetry embraces both sacred and secular themes, and a strong vein of socio-political comment runs through her work.

ACKNOWLEDGEMENTS

'Mother's Day' in *Canberra Times*,
Saturday 10 May 2003, Panorama.
'Isa' in *Australian Islamic Review*, vol 7,
issue 12, December 2002.
'Intifada' in *Australian Islamic Review*, vol 7,
issue 5, May 2002.
'Maghrib Journey' in *Australian Islamic
Review*, vol 7, issue 6, June 2002.
'Zikr' in *The Muslim Woman*, (Nigeria)
issue no 7, 2000.
'Strike on Iraq' (poem previously published as
'Desert Strike' in Nigeria in *The Muslim
Woman*, issue no 7, 2000) in *Australian Islamic
Review*, vol 8, issue 3, March 2003.

I would like to sincerely thank my husband
and children, for their support in my writing.
Thanks also to Elizabeth Mansutti for her
perceptive comments on this collection and
its title.

*These poems are dedicated to Graham Rowlands
and Graeme Webster.*

CONTENTS

Amanda's Wedding

Women wore fox furs and jewels,
one backless to the waist,
despite the cold
with bouffant hair like a camel's hump.
Amanda cut the ribbon
and led us up red carpeted stairs.
Saints with gilded haloes
recognised from Sunday school,
frozen in their stories
adorned the walls inside.
The choir chanted an anthem as
we gazed transfixed at the screen.
The voyeur camera focussed
on Amanda's face and breast,
wandered over the guests
but always zoomed back
to her red smile.
The patriarch crowned the bridegroom,
held a gold crown above
Amanda's coiffured hair-
its dark blond betrayed Greek origins –
and tied a red ribbon around her neck.
Triumphant they progressed the aisle.
Outside they shook our hands
in a formal, family line.

At the Meridian's foyer we waited
until Amanda waltzed to Strauss,
played by a few violins.
Upstairs I longed for dinner
but another waltz recorded
their progress on video.

Then alcohol flowed inside
as the Nile flowed outside.
The white tiered cake glowed fluorescent
pink, blue, orange, green and yellow.
A belly dancer swayed
above the enthroned couple,
enhanced by smoke and coloured lights.
The banquet was rushed –
we found only leftovers.
Amanda and her husband
had fed each other cake.
They feasted on each other
while the porter ate beans.

Mother's Day

I smell the white chrysanthemums
and put on my black headscarf.
It's Mother's Day – but you lie
beneath Greek soil; wild thyme
adorns your grave, perfumes the air,
where goats run down the mountain side
behind a barefoot boy
near the Aegean sea.

I want to give you these flowers,
Mama, but it's too far.
Instead I'll go to where Antonio rests,
under the shady gums,
a rosary
for you both
and these blossoms
placed beneath that simple stone
where trains pass by.

Peter

Sunflowers remind me of you,
and red patches in your canvases like Van Gogh.
I thought of his brown and yellow flowers
when I placed mine on your grave –
the taxi played Vincent
en route to your funeral.
Your talent eclipsed mine.
Only paintings, drawings and lithographs remain;
a narrow plot, simple cross and memories
reaching back to your birth
when I counted your fingers and toes.
Now your body and bluish ears outrage me.

Blood of my blood, sweat of my sweat,
you left us to swallow our tears.
Then you lay like a statue
dressed in new clothes,
smiling like Lenin,
but when I touched your shirt
plastic moved under my fingers.
The undertaker's arm
didn't console me.
I needed to feel you alive –
muscles taut, nerves quivering
and warm skin –
instead of that formaldehyde dummy.

Isa

My Jesus is called Isa.
He does not have blue eyes and blond hair,
like the one in Sunday School.
He has no sacred heart, nor crown of thorns,
nor wounded side. He has no cross.
By God's grace he healed the sick, raised the dead,
and spoke in his cradle,
but he never said
'Worship me.'

Now I yearn for haj –
veiled in a bus for Mecca,
carried forward by the crowd
to see the sacred place and kiss
the black stone.

Now I love Isa more as a man
who shared our human frailties
than a mythical son of God.
Now I know Allah is One.
Although I cannot see Him,
He sees me and is nearer than the vein in my neck,
and Isa is close to Him.
My Jesus is called Isa.

Breath of Allah

Oranges hang over my back door
a blade of grass, green scimitar,
curves towards light.
The sun sets over dark hills
like a scene from a Hollywood movie.
A semi-circular moon glows
on black velvet sky
behind palm fronds as crickets chirp.
Allah, you are the force
that flows through all things –
the source of life you breathed into man.
With every breath the Sufi says 'Allah'.
The world is a breath of Allah.

Intifada

The star of David crushed
the entwined circles
when Sharon went to Temple Mount.
Missiles smashed buildings and homes.
Trees were uprooted
and people hemmed in like Jews
from a Warsaw ghetto.
Young boys threw stones at tanks
like David attacking Goliath.
We watch these gladiators,
like modern day Romans,
from armchairs instead of arenas
between cups of tea and coffee.

Haiku

Scaffolding forest
hiding jagged minarets,
dome appears golden.

Goats sit on the road
traffic jam, crowds converge:
Jum'ah prayer call.

Dust on my forehead
dust on thousands of foreheads:
Sallah Day again.

Chechnya

A lone sniper fights his last battle
from a clock tower –
elsewhere his comrades surrender.
Terrified civilians huddle
among the rubble in freezing cold,
dreading murder or rape.

Many rebels are blown apart
but some escape to the mountains.
They know every inch, every rock
of their land.
As long as men are born
Russian soldiers will beware
the boy behind a tree,
the girl with a basket,
the knife that slices flesh,
the night ambush,
the cratered site
where once a building stood.
They cannot win guerrilla war.

Civilians aren't counted
and every week a Russian soldier dies here.

Maghrib Journey

Allah, I feel your Presence near
under the vastness of the sky,
in the grey hills of the horizon,
and in the flaming orb that lights the west
as clouds darken the east
above earth's rounded mounds
and in the luxuriant growth
that flourishes green-yellow
through the dusk.

I feel it in the rosy hue
when the sun has slipped away
darkening the sky, where red fades
near the earth's edge,
silhouetting trees
while the first star glows
as night descends.

Prayer for Peace

Kosovo bled while the Ummah* slept.
Now we pray for peace, O Lord,
peace for this ravaged land.
Grant bliss to the martyrs;
solace the orphans,
widows and dishonoured women.
Shelter the homeless.
Heal their wounds, O Lord,
bring peace to Kosovo.
Let it bloom upon this blood-soaked soil
like a rose in paradise –
a rose that has no thorns.

*The world-wide community of Muslims

Zikr

Behind my eyelids glows golden –
Allah, you own everything.
You make the date seed split and sprout,
the sky pour rain upon parched soil.
Your presence envelopes the heavens and earth
You tire not to maintain.
I glimpse infinity, Majesty Most High –
for a second after Friday prayer.

Bida Mosque

As I peered through the lattice,
a forest of green soared through my tears.
I prayed Asr prayer
then explored the mosque.
A crystal chandelier sparkled,
under the dome,
shining with gold leaf,
I craned my neck to see Ayat – ul – kirsi
dance around its base.
Small chandeliers hung like flowers
between green columns.
One word – Allah – dominated the wall
where the imam would pray.
Space echoed vast, empty,
except for a few workers
where later many heads would bow,
and I thanked God
for Bida Mosque.

Strike on Iraq

Green light flickers the screen
as bombs explode Baghdad.
My country is at war
with my adopted country.
My brothers and sisters in faith
mourn their dead,
while chaotic images
destroy my peace of mind.
I cry, helpless, before ads
for human rights.

Night of Power

Beneath us stood rows
of men behind the imam
whose hands, like ours, supplicated
before their breasts.
As the dua went on and on
my legs ached, but I would not sit down.
My chest expanded with joy
although I knew only
a few words – as if I listened to
a divine opera.
Ya Allah (O Allah)
chanted the imam with passion,
standing in the minbar niche
recessed into a painting of the Kaba
and it seemed as if
I, too, were there, among the throng
I'd only seen before on TV.
Then for a moment I felt a part
of those multitudes around the world
who pray to One God.

Dawn Prayer

I slipped from the quilt
into the cool dawn.
The ninety nine names of Allah
ran like pearls though my fingers.
I stood, bowed, touched my forehead
to the mat.
I searched for my Beloved
and found Him in my prayer.
Like Rabi'ah*, I am the doorkeeper
of my heart.
I keep the world from getting in
and the inside from getting out
until I am His
and all is One.

*Rabi'ah al-Adawiyyah (717–801) was an early
female Sufi who wrote poetry and prayers.

Out of Africa

Today everything looks new,
as if I saw Fulani cattle
for the first time,
because we're leaving them
behind.

Now I see these frangipani trees
anew, and sheets, towels and curtains
pegged out for sale in Kaduna
like washing on a line.
And I remember other trips here
in other days
and I wonder how long before
I too come,
out of Africa.

Africa, my Africa

Harmattan* mists, dry grass,
and mud huts
like those I first saw
from the plane with fresh eyes –
a tourist on a working holiday.
Then everything seemed easy, plain
until the humdrum took over.

Boys walk in file, carrying baskets.
Hawkers crowd the car
pushing yoghurt, apples
and fried plantain inside.
Smoke rises above savannah scrub –
large vistas, empty spaces
except for the odd trader selling yam
and a woman bowed under
a load of firewood.

Gum trees stand serene
reminding me of home,
but this was also home for twenty years,
experience deep inside of
fever and dysentery
side by side with memories
of courtship, wedding and family,
Sallah rams, durbahs and naming ceremonies.
Here the crescent moon caught me
under her spell.

Our daughters backed babies,
cooked pounded yam,
and danced for joy with their black friend
under our palm tree's lattice,
cleaning paint buckets, pouring watery 'milk'
into puddles, drenching their olive skin.
They also beat the rhythm
for their birthday musical chairs
on an upturned plastic bowl.

I too ate pounded yam,
but now I crave familiar food and faces
so this bittersweet life must end.
Yet something else must linger on
inside the blood, not only parasites
but Africa, Africans.

*Harmattan is a season in Nigeria between the wet and
dry seasons, characterised by cool, misty mornings,
when the wind blows sand from the Sahara desert.

Harmattan meets Global Warming

Fulani cattle wander patiently
across arid savannah.
Villages sleep in the sun
where palm trees rise majestic
above stunted scrub.
A woman treks bowed under
a load of firewood.
Cars stop at mini markets where
bundles of dry wood line the road.

Yellow grasses and mist
whisper of harmattan,
while cracked heels yearn for Vaseline.
Dust covers everything
as sand invades the sheets.

The land, already scorched in places
by man-made fires burning off dried grass,
thirsts for rain –
the cycle never changes.
But this year and last
heat bakes the dust
banishing cool nights and mornings
into the small hours
of mist.

Rainy Season in Nigeria

Fulani cattle roam
across lush savannah
where odd boulders dot scrub –
some huge mounds worn smooth
by countless rains.

Goats frolic on rocks among emerald hills,
while slate grey clouds loom overhead
ready with rain.
This green reminds me of England,
even winter in South Australia.
Yet there are no gum trees here,
nor purple wildflowers –
only the unmarked mounds of a Muslim graveyard.
Will my bones rest under these tufts –
or will I smell the gums' fragrance again,
and walk under southern skies?

Among the Debris

Here we sort among the debris –
books, papers, saucepans
odds and ends –
like relatives after the funeral,
only you phoned last night
after we were here.
Dust covers everything
except your clothes in the closet
and some china in a cupboard,
making me wheeze,
tightening my breath.
I seized your rusty cruet
with one decanter lost,
for oil or vinegar,
because it reminded me of home.
The silent rocking horse stands still
behind the couch,
where once our children used to play.

Next door the garden's gravelled
but green riot covers pebbles
where people steal your mangoes,
and wild hedge spills
inside the garden.

A carpet of dried, brown leaves
under the rusting boat
spreads to the roofless gazebo
where we ate together.
Only the ghosts of the past
eat there now.
Only the lake and luxuriant,
emerald hills remain the same
as we sort through the debris,
the remnants of your lives –
and ours.

Sallah Ram

The ram's blood spurted
from its jugular
as I jumped away.
I had to watch this sacrifice –
which atones for my sins,
but it's hard
because I didn't grow up with it.
So I left the butchering –
the slaughtered ram, eyes glazed,
head lolling in a pool of blood –
to go back into
the warmth and safety of our kitchen
where the meat arrived
neatly parcelled for the freezer.

Designer Jacket

Your designer jacket sways
around your hips
as you stride the mall
on high heels.
Your crushed flower oils,
your musk wafts the autumn warmth.
You sit, legs crossed, sip Cappuccino,
a boutique package by your feet
your body firm from the gym.
I suppose you know and don't know
how some migrant woman sweated
until midnight,
framed behind the clatter
of an oiled Singer
for a dollar or two an hour,
sandwiched between meals, chores, and children
so you could wear that jacket?

Tokyo Lecher

Kaori peels her school uniform off nubile limbs . . .
Later, your wife greets you with rice, fish and tea –
her almond eyes plead for your approval.
You'll accept these offerings like a god,
this apartment your shrine, a chrysanthemum
before your wedding photo, your daughter –
a treasure,
how does she afford
fashion clothes, designer handbags, shoes,
    a mobile phone?
While you serve your company,
fathers and grandfathers take your treasure
as you take Kaori.

Tattoo

Blue rose wrapped around a sword,
forever on his arm.
Pretty girl, with spider on belly button,
what if she tires of it?

Nigerians have their own tattoos –
tribal marks on black faces,
gouged by the knife
on a baby's skin.
Before the white man
these marks identified –
they'd fight or be welcomed.

What if we had tattoos
to show
friend or foe?

SCOFFING GNOCCHI

by Linda Uphill

Linda Uphill was born in Mount Gambier
and moved to Adelaide in 2000. She has been
scribbling poems in her diary since she began
high school. Inspiration has often come
during lectures, when she can't find a pen, or
in the night when she'd pawn her nostrils for
some sleep. She loves fairy bread, ginger,
woollen socks and waiting for ducklings to
cross South Road. She hates American soaps
and cabbage. She has recently completed a
Bachelor of Arts at the University of South
Australia majoring in Professional Writing.

ACKNOWLEDGEMENTS

'Delight yourself in the LORD and He will
give you the desires of your heart'
Psalm 37:4

Thank you to Amelia Walker for inspiring me
more than you could know,
to Garry Costello, the most wonderful teacher,
I will never forget you
to Ioana Petrescu,
to Mum and Dad,
and Rowan for all your encouragement

for Nana and Grandad

CONTENTS

Dumb falung

baby elephants
stand on cement
eating bananas
in the narrow streets
of Bangkok
they press against merchants
who sit crosslegged on bright rugs
with their rich crops of bangles,
beads and incense sticks
i eat sweet mango and rice
squeeze between small bodies
into the market place
'you large' they boom blankfaced,
i feel wounded
and throw my sweet mango in the bin

i step into the day
where diseased chooks and dogs
with ugly lumps hanging
pass painfully by monks
and mandarin sellers
and bangs of meat drip, rotting in the sun
my took-took raises itself
onto its hind legs
like a pony

i scream
as we charge towards a bus
and the driver spins a head on his shoulder
cries, 'me champion took-took!'
and all i can do is think wildly
my mother'd kill you, as i grit my teeth

clipping cars,
my eyes catch frames of girls,
young girls dressed in red
with long black plaits
who hang on arms of westerners
like hair wrapped round thick fingers
a family rides by on a motorbike
a mother, a father, a child
and the groceries
they point at my red curls
and laugh
they laugh
at the silly fat falung
so dumb
who just doesn't understand

Caged

*Written for a friend whose family
fled from Afghanistan and sought
refuge in Australia in 2001*

She was a bright child
Humming educate me
She was one child in a sea
That shook
Eight of them locked in a room
Below deck,
Never seeing the sun
No food
Squeezing eyes tight
While the baby cried
Pressing into each other
Into memories
Of orchards, fresh fish
And fattened calves
In a world filled with terror
Where they stole her brother
And locked her in a room,
Never seeing the sun
Whispering in the dark

Being educated
By a man who would be
Locked in a room,
Never seeing the sun
Who would flee from them
And his children would cry
And arrive.
To be locked in a room,
Never seeing the sun
They sat on their beds
Too frightened to speak
As our country
Expressed its compassion

Eighteen

an erratic mood has him in a strangle hold
he moves like a man possessed by
some inner force that will not let him relax
or sit still and it pushes his
eyebrows down over his eyes
he mentioned an x-ray they took of his head
pretty unsatisfactory but it must be enough
for i gave him dark peppermint chocolate
as i glided out of his car

they're all sitting in a windowless room
talking we-got-all-this-spiritual-shit-worked-out
and i cant even say have you forgotten me
you bastards
come paint me special again

he speaks into the whites of my eyes how
he cannot remember his childhood
it comes in flashes and spits of light
with faces and expressions frozen in time
and i'm looking round for someone to see me
but their faces are elsewhere inclined

i run away to where the slugs are gorging on
cat food and spiders hiss and strike my feet
and i listen to them scream at God
i listen to them speak and feel the halo rise
from my knees where it trips me
all affections are wound about others
and he's wretched and looking at me

we have so many tears for ourselves
we just want to get a bottle of scotch
and swim in it till we grow tired and drown
they listen but none of them care
they're not forgiving me for myself
and he is here reaching for my hand
assuring me of worth i've come to question

they're vomiting in distress
i make such a good shoulder i wonder that
i wasn't born one
they're bouncing like deer when they're happy
they're swelling with the power
that bottles the sea
they're speaking and it's too hot for words
they're melting in their mouths
i'm weary of their mouths
they stimulate the mind
when they don't exhaust it
i'm collapsing he's catching me
he's caught me
i drive home and i cannot see for my tears
you see when there is no one looking
and there are no words
you have to refresh yourself somewhere

i feel caged which is funny
i always thought i wanted one
and they're accusing me with their hands on
   their hips

i'm living with a tornado in my chest!
and i'm hating them for this
breaking me before him and i'm resenting every
inch of their bodies and beings
hoping they'll call my name

nails digging out great holes
drillings through me boring through my whole body
hurting – this spiked marble pushing at me

they're scoffing gnocchi pomodori
kissing me with their backs
a never ending reproach

you can't teach that

now my gut green with it
my gut is green
you can stretch your eyeballs
but this is *mine* and you cannot have it
this was the perfect example of boiling restraint
i thought i had conquered my demons
but they're still clawing away at my brain
a sense of loss, a dark anger and a grief like fire
in my belly streaming into my fists and to my legs
fuelling them with violence

he's stroking my hair and strangling me
and my gut is green with the fishes

Thank you

I have nothing to touch
just a voice
speaking tender
making it hard
I push my head closer
and the words ripple purplic
in warm rich twists.
I shine
when you make me

reach.

Selling cellulite

I wish I could sell cellulite
Then I could fly first-class
I'd parade through Venice, Greece and Spain
Swinging my sexy slim arse

I'd bag it like potpourri
And sell it by the pound
They'd use it to make candles
And pimple cream, no doubt

Oh I could make a fortune
If the market weren't so weak
If I could sell my cellulite
I could live off my pure cheek!

Shaggy farmhouse

Summer.
The shaggy old farmhouse
Stands, half beautiful
Amongst the dry stalks.
Fat black flies
Storm the chimney
In fat black waves
Wheedling through wires
Squirting maggot pips
In writhing piles
Dirtying ledges as they die.
We smash them.

Winter.
The shaggy old farmhouse
Pants in the storm
Offers its head to be drummed by the rain.
The bright wet grass
Sprouts daffodils
And dark monsters lurk in
Cradled, cracked wood.
The soothe of the blaze and
Of chilled fingers on cups
Is slain by the scream
As they creep . . . slyly
Too big to smash.

Moon

fragrance of closeness
the beauty of wildflowers
in the pillowlight

Dancing in the dairy

he moves her,
embracing, in out to
himself,
skillfully navigating
her frame through the
torrent of sloppy poo
and torrential yellow rain

New
Haiku

Trembling new limbs slide
A small pink mouth seeks calming
From the bright yellow

New II
Free verse

Thin little legs are bobbing
It is cold
New limbs are wavering
The thick red-black curtain
Moved soundlessly, opening
The world
It is cold
A small pink mouth seeks comfort
As she shakes
Blinking big bewildered eyes
At the bright yellow

This place

In this place
I hate my memories

Despite the revving utes and
discarded bundy cans –
behind young wincing eyes
and aggressive crotch displays
beneath the VB caps
between the twisted smiles

I see
innocence is splashing crazy-happy in the air
I want to open my mouth –
      gargle
until my tongue feels clean
      again
until my brain glows mint

I look at them
young girls shyly survey small boys
the boys stand together
hands in pockets
girls whisper and giggle
they're all so excited
are we going out now?
should I wait
should he come up to me?
should I hold his hand?
The air's awash with orange
and the taste of secrets

Fruit Cate

She's an anxious driver girl
licking for a smash.
She hurts them all can't shake the
feeling
she's been short changed.
She knows all of it…
Santa sold out to Coca-Cola
the North Pole is melting
and Noddy is gay.
She knows garbage when she hears it,
seethes with arctic fury
at how controlled she's been
says,
'When I open my mouth,
I can't even scream!
I've got nits, I'm angry, I'm ugly!
No war in my name!'
She remembers dreaming, dreaming
it smelt like sweat and looked like pearls.
They ate spaghetti and meatballs
by bottled candlelight, in the cold –
talked about sex and surfing,
a crew of excitement soaked in champagne.
Splashing in the sauna –
dizzied through lack of sleep,
stuffing fistfulls of choc chips inside
their happy, flapping mouths . . .

And now –
older, smarter, more cynical
she gags on politician's words
won't read the paper anymore –
it reminds her she is small.

This isn't what they promised
when she graduated

Last Summer

On the first day of Summer
I closed my eyes
and dreamed
of passionfruit

of its big moist belly
soft-pocked with shining yellow seed

I dreamed of carving it out
and letting the smooth tang
slip down
inside my throat

sunshine lit the fringes of my dream
with squiggling yellow cracks
and Summer flickered my split ends
I opened my eyes
I'm in love
and then

He's here

I close my eyes
and dream
of passionfruit

Skin

peeling back your skin
i'd dwell inside your stomach
you would be my world

The tragedy of Katherine

The girl stood there.
It looked like she was offering
herself to the world.
She flung her head into the traffic
arms outstretched
brown pigtails and bright red flairs
a giant smile
chest pushed out by her deep breath
eyelids sunned by the dazzle.

Years on now,
the old woman keeps a
cradle by her bed,
presses a plastic doll to her breast;
she burps the ugly, poker-faced
ghost
rocks it, knits it booties
and weans it in the silence
of her house.

Death

Death
You wave that red hot banner
You roar and you petrify
They tremble at your approach

O Death
Where did you go?
Where has your sting been spat to?

O Accuser
O Flatterer
O Liar

Do you feel a little cheated?

How is it that your fearsome oath signals
Nothing
That your blistering stare
Is now . . .

Irrelevant.

Held

Nailing jelly to the walls –
– My broken, unfocused prayers,
Your cursor on my head –
The temptation to despair
Record *me*
Old church
Shaving shells
Record *me*
Cold cocoa
As I serenade your toes

No point keeping this inside

The whipping tongue against my conscience
The terrified grief and the cracking of cheeks
The smashing against my sense of being

I take the sense of who I am from you
When I feel the
                    bite
I'm the people proud of you
Overwhelmed by you
Feel my heart filled by a vision of you

And I'm scribbling down a whispering

A cup of tea with Jesus

If I were quiet one whole second
would you come?
and if I acted perfectly, would
you lie down next to me?

I'd be sleeping
could you hold me just a minute
do you think?
or should I shake your hand –
ignore the scars?
Would you come to the pub with me,
could we get a beer?
Could we forget how I neglect you?
Would you help me dye my hair?
Could I massage your brown shoulders,
till you smiled?

Should I vacuum, dust and polish?
Should I hire jugglers, acrobats,
thespians and choirs?
Could we make a holy sound
to make you pleased?
or
could we sit quietly
sipping
saying nothing
and have a cup of tea?

The girl and the night

Loss
It was a hurting, hot night
she bled into the bruised sky
smeared purple blue
and sore
she wept into the tomato froth
stirred, bone tragic
eating nothing but ginger nuts
banishing thoughts of a face.

Beauty
This night was smooth
dark liquid cream
with that crazy wind that
         floats in
from dream places
swinging cool, then warm
she was breathing in baileys
smelling people unknown
feeling young.
He twirls her about in his fingertips
huge hands, blackened nails
spins her fragile waist
through pollen, lanterns, lavender incense
and frothy top mugs
past the milk moustaches
and the french eloise
she shimmers as he whirls her through
the café house
into the night.

Love
Dark night
skittles sliding through her
swimming and blending
a rainbow river
river-hot,
flowing, bleeding into the walls
like soaking in vodka
then
a fireworks display in her stomach.

For this I am grateful

My Catherine wheel,
Opalescent one
You make a mawker out of me
You splash of bright
You *tiny freak*

this is yours
for Jennifer

this music.
the way you sing.
you hit
your head against formula
redlined as you move
to the music in your eye.
she swings her body
to sound
and cries.

Then

Two nights ago the sunset was soft
and the sky golden tanned as I sat
in the fish and chip shop massacring
my ticket and listening to the sound of
the chips cooking and the
oil sizzling and spitting

The land turned bright navy and the
houses were like stars, forming
an endless sky
and the moon was
a mighty orange
burning away in the darkness

But
without him
I felt like just another person
watching something beautiful

For more information visit www.wakefieldpress.com.au